Save
The Owls

by Jeri Lee C.Ht.

ISBN: 9798356244476

Sample Page

Sample Page

Author
Jeri Lee C.Ht.

Hailed for their supposed wisdom and appetite for pesky rodents but derided as pests and subjects of superstition, owls (Tytonidae and Strigidae) have had a love/hate relationship with humans since the beginning of recorded history. There are over 200 species of owls, which might date back to the days of dinosaurs. About 216 species of owls are divided into two families: Barn and Bay (Tytonidae) and Strigidae (true owls). Most owls belong to the so-called true owls, with large heads, round faces, short tails, and muted feathers with mottled patterns. The remaining dozen-plus species are barn owls, which have heart-shaped faces, long legs with powerful talons, and moderate size. Except for the common barn owl, which is found worldwide, the most familiar owls in North America and Eurasia are the true owls.

More than half of the owls in the world live in the neotropics and sub-Saharan Africa, and only 19 species reside in the United States and Canada.

One of the most remarkable things about owls is that they move their entire heads when looking at something rather than moving their eyes, like most other vertebrates. Owls need large, forward-facing eyes to gather scarce light during their nocturnal hunts, and evolution couldn't spare the musculature to allow these eyes to rotate. Some owls have astonishingly flexible necks that let them turn their heads three-quarters of a circle, or 270 degrees, compared to 90 degrees for the average human.This coloring book is designed especially for adults and teens. It comprises high-quality coloring pages for enthusiastic participants with creative minds and happy pencils. With a few flowers and butterflies added for a pinch of color, it should be a delight for any adult or teen that loves beauty in their entertainment. It belongs to a series of coloring books primarily focused on saving our planet. Yor can be creative and add the sun with a few clouds for shades in your backgrounds of blue and gold. You now have a project suitable for framing.

With respect for our planet and the disrespect of how its population has treated it either knowingly or unconsciously, I believe we all share the guilt of its destruction and the responsibility of its rescue. I share with you the echoing voices of two of its most recent authorities on the subject and pledge to do my part in helping the planet help itself.

This Book
Belongs to

____

Your Name

____

Date

SAVE THE
PLANET

LET THERE BE PEACE ON EARTH AND LET IT BEGIN WITH ME

OUR FUTURE
IS IN
OUR HANDS

SAVE THE EARTH

Save our Planet

SAVE THE BEES

SAVE OUR
PLANET

OCT
4TH
World
Animal Day
Save The
Amazon

SAVE
OCEAN

SAVE
THE
SEA

WORLD
TURTLE DAY

SAVE THE EARTH

OUR FUTURE
IS IN
OUR HANDS

LET THERE
BE PEACE
ON EARTH
AND
LET IT BEGIN
WITH ME

World
Wildlife
Day

save the BEES

SAVE THE PLANET

SAVE THE
KOALA
DAY
SEPTEMBER 24

SAVE
THE
BEES

SAVE THE WILDLIFE
OF AFRICA

KEEP the OCEAN
CLEAN

LET THERE BE PEACE ON EARTH
AND LET IT BEGIN WITH ME

save the planet

SAVE THE PLANET
SAVE OURSELVES

Save the
BEES

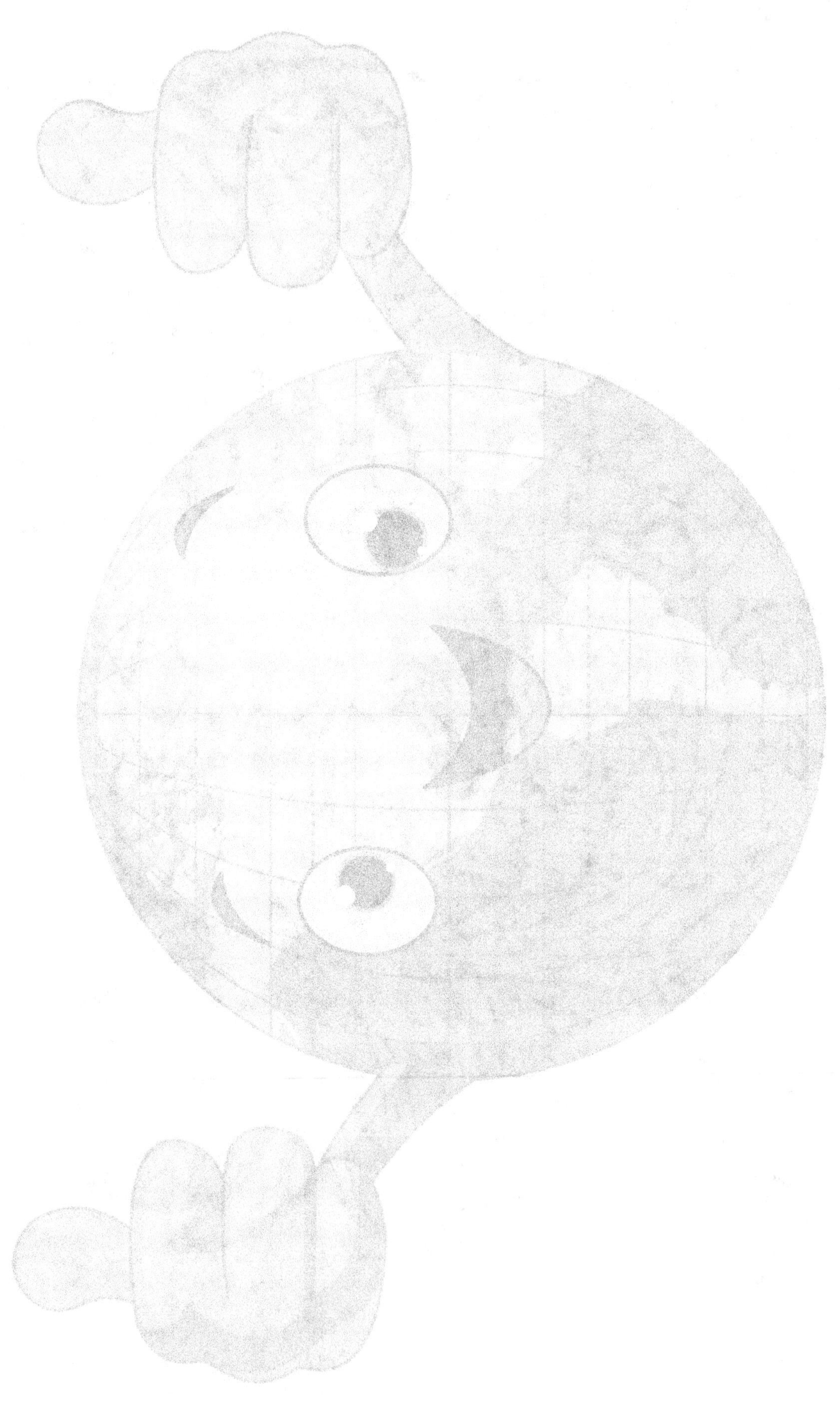

KEEP the OCEAN CLEAN

save
the world!

Too
hot

WORLD TURTLE DAY

MAY 23

African Elephant

Asian Elephant

You Might Enjoy

Other Coloring Books

Save the Planet Series
Family Pets Series
Match the Colors Series
Fantasy Series
Flowers & Birds Series
Adult Coloring Book Series

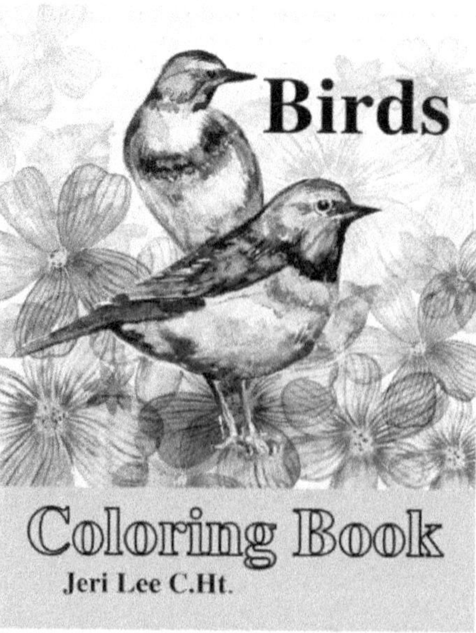

Author
and
Artist
Jeri LeeC.Ht.

Early education is fundamental for the children in our life. The ABCs and 1-2-3s we teach them are the building blocks of their future. We first give them love and care. Then we teach them to walk and talk and right from wrong. Next is their formal education and how to socialize in their environment. It is here that my books can assist. As a mother, grandmother, and great-grandmother, I know that all kids relate to animals, and the first ones they meet are their household pets. Then as they venture out, they meet Farm animals and learn new words like duck, pig, horses, and cows, and they soon discover the habits, sounds, and colors of their new friends. Then a visit to the Zoo introduces them to the world of Nature, and it is essential to teach them to respect without touching our natural environment.

I grew up on a farm and have lived on one most of my life, so it's a subject that comes easy. My coloring books are designed to teach kids to respect the world they live in.

They are published in collectible series with different coloring pages for different ages and interests.

If you like this book, please follow my other series, and if you would give me a good review as an author, I would greatly appreciate it.

UNIVERSAL

PEACE